101 HOCKEY JOKES

Kara Woodburn

illustrations by
Bill Dickson

Scholastic Canada Ltd.
Toronto New York London Auckland Sydney
Mexico City New Delhi Hong Kong Buenos Aires

Scholastic Canada Ltd.
604 King Street West, Toronto, Ontario M5V 1E1, Canada

Scholastic Inc.
557 Broadway, New York, NY 10012, USA

Scholastic Australia Pty Limited
PO Box 579, Gosford, NSW 2250, Australia

Scholastic New Zealand Limited
Private Bag 94407, Botany, Manukau 2163, New Zealand

Scholastic Children's Books
Euston House, 24 Eversholt Street, London NW1 1DB, UK

Library and Archives Canada Cataloguing in Publication
Woodburn, Kara
101 hockey jokes / by Kara Woodburn ; illustrations by Bill Dickson.
ISBN 978-1-4431-1333-5
1. Hockey--Juvenile humor. 2. Canadian wit and humor (English).
I. Dickson, Bill II. Title. III. Title: One hundred and one hockey jokes.
PN6231.H54W66 2012   j796.96202'07   C2011-908094-X

6 5 4 3 2 1   Printed in Canada 116   12 13 14 15 16

To my family and friends who
are always on my team!
And to Ron,
who makes me laugh.

What does a winning team drink at breakfast?

A *Stanley Cup* of coffee!

Why was the hockey player's cake so plain?

He forgot the icing!

Why was there a delay at airport security?

All the hockey players were getting checked!

What does a hockey player do on vacation?

He takes a breakaway!

What hot beverage do enforcers drink?

*Penal*tea!

What does a hockey player
put on top of his sundae?

A Don Cherry!

Why was the hockey player cold all the time?

He was number one in the draft!

What do a hockey player and a magician have in common?

Hat tricks!

Why did the hockey player open
a Tim Hortons?

He was a franchise player!

Why was the goalie late for
practice?

*She was having dinner with
friends at the cross*bar!

Which hockey player really needs to clean his room?

Mark Messier!

Where did the goalie like
to shop?

Any place he could save!

Who was the teacher's favourite
hockey player?

The one who kept passing!

What do you call a hockey player lying on his back or front?

*Off*side!

What do you call a hockey player when he's lying on his stomach?

Back*up!*

What do you call a
chicken playing hockey?

A *goal*tender!

Why do Toronto's players always think they're going to win the Stanley Cup?

Because they beLeaf in themselves!

Why did the hockey player take up javelin throwing?

He liked high-sticking!

Why did the offensive coach get frustrated when he checked his email?

He had too many forwards!

Why did the goalie on a losing streak have such long arms?

The coach kept pulling him!

Why couldn't fans recognize the star forward?

He had his faceoff!

What do you call a hockey tournament for birds?

A round robin!

What do you call a hockey player who loses his house keys?

A shutout!

Why did the police officer think the right winger was a thief?

He had possession of the puck!

Why did the hockey player limp when he walked?

He had a toe drag.

Why did the hockey player take up fishing?

He was good at hooking!

How do the Canadiens get to the Bell Centre?

They take Hab *rides!*

Why did the hockey player go to court?

To plead to the goal judge!

How does a hockey player watch a movie at home?

She presses power play!

Why was the hockey player not "It" when he was tagged?

He was in the neutral zone!

What is a hockey player's favourite dairy product?

Top cheese!

What's a cowboy's favourite part of a hockey game?

The shootouts!

29

Why were the parents banned from the game?

They were smothering the puck!

What is a hockey player's least favourite dessert?

A turnover!

What kind of hats do hockey players hate to wear?

Salary caps!

Why did the new goalie bring a pen to practice?

He was told he'd be given hockey pads!

What do you call rodents
that play hockey?

Rink rats!

Why did the Zamboni driver call a plumber?

Because the ice was flooded!

What kind of art does Edmonton have in its locker room?

Oiler paintings!

What do you call a hockey player who writes scripts?

*A play*maker*!*

Why don't goalies get sunburned at the beach?

They wear blockers!

What is a hockey player's least favourite part of an airplane ride?

Boarding!

How did the hockey player pay for his cool new clothes?

With a hip cheque!

Why did the hockey player get a promotion at work?

Because she worked overtime!

What do you call a hockey
player who loves fruit?

A cherry picker!

What did the hockey player do
when the weather got warmer?

He dropped his gloves!

How do goalies hunt?

With a net!

41

Why were the team's gloves too big?

They were short-handed!

What do you call a group of players that keeps gaining weight?

An expansion team!

What does a bird do before he gives up the puck?

Feathers the pass!

Why did the hockey player believe in aliens?

He kept seeing saucer passes!

What do you call hockey players from the country?

A farm team!

How do you know which hockey players dye their hair?

They're on the highlight reel!

How does a hockey player know when a girl likes him?

He gets called up!

What do you call a hockey player who serves in the army?

Major Penalty!

Why was the hockey team arrested?

They killed the clock!

What do you call a hockey player who borrows his equipment?

A rental player!

Why are hockey players so
messy?

*Because they have scrumbs
everywhere!*

Why do hockey players like
giving autographs?

Because they get signing bonuses!

Why was the hockey player
on crutches?

Because she hurt her shinny!

What do you say to an Ottawa player who has nice handwriting?

"Great Sensmanship!"

Why do hockey players pick up sewing so easily?

They already know how to thread the needle!

When do hockey players
dress in formal attire?

When it's a tie game!

What did the girl hockey stick
say to the boy hockey stick?

Puck*er up!*

What did the coach say after
he took his defencemen out for
dinner?

Check please!

What do you call a hockey player who drives a boat?

The captain!

Why did the hockey puck quit the team?

It was tired of being slapped!

Where do coaches get sent
when they misbehave?

To the Coach's Corner!

What do you get when you hire a pig at an arena?

A ham*boni driver!*

Why was the hockey player so quick to stand up for himself?

He was a defence*man!*

What do you call a hockey player who swats bees?

A buzzer beater!

What is another term for a hockey fan?

Canadian!

Why can't knights play hockey?

They keep getting penalties for spearing.

What do you call a hockey player who shows no fear?

Toothless!

What do the coach's home renovations and team practices have in common?

They both have lots of drills!

Why is it always so cold in hockey arenas?

Because there are lots of fans!

What do you call it when hockey players try to get dates on the ice?

Pickup hockey!

What do you call a hockey player without a stick?

A figure skater!

Why did the hockey player call 911 when his shot was blocked?

Because he was robbed!

What do an outdoor ice rink and a rookie have in common?

They can both crack under pressure!

Where do you send someone who doesn't like hockey?

To the Hall of Lame!

Why did the hockey player get kicked out of art class?

She drew a penalty!

Who is the prickliest hockey player in the league?

The one with the most points!

Which team has the strongest swimmers?

The San Jose Sharks!

Why did the pig have to sit out the game?

He'd pulled a ham*string!*

What do you call a hockey player after he escapes jail?

A breakout player!

Why did the hockey player go to the doctor?

For a check up!

What do you call a hockey player who watches what he says?

A mouth guard!

Why do athletes love to play hockey in Canada?

Because it's cooler here!

What did the hockey player use as a paddle?

A Bobby Orr!

Which Canadian team has the best dance moves?

Vangroover!

What is Wayne Gretzky's favourite bakery?

The Great Bun!

What's it called when a player is kicked out of a game for not wearing pants?

*Un*shorts*manlike conduct*!

Knock, knock.

Who's there?

Winna.

Winna who?

Winna-peg, but I want to win a Stanley Cup!

Why was the puck so heavy?

Because everyone kept trying to feed it.

Why did the hockey player love chicken so much?

Because he was a wingman!

What do you call an unemployed hockey player?

A stay-at-home defenceman!

When do hockey players send most of their mail?

In the post season!

Knock, knock.

Who's there?

Gordie.

Gordie who?

*Gordie Howe do you not know
who I am?*

Where can you find flames
on ice?

At the Calgary Saddledome!

What do you call a hockey player in outer space?
An all-star!